What They're Saying...

"If you are interested in developing your leadership skills, Cory Dobbs' new book, *Leadership Quest* is the place to start. This is the perfect guide for young athletes just starting their leadership journey or veteran athletes seeking to get back on the right track as a leader. Asking the reader to consider the tough questions and providing action steps critical to success, Cory's message is straightforward and relentless."
  - *Kathy Delaney-Smith, Women's Basketball Coach, Harvard University*

Brilliant in its simplicity yet rich in its message, this inspiring and empowering fable by Cory Dobbs illuminates the soulful path of athletic leadership and what it means not just for sports but for all of life. I will be recommending this book to all of my student-athletes aspiring to discover their true leader within. Cory's insights on leadership are extraordinary as this book will demonstrate.
  - *Dr. Jerry Lynch, Sport Psychologist, Author of Creative Coaching and founder of Way of the Champions*

Without a doubt a key element to getting anyone to become willing and able to be a good leader is for the person to develop the "mindset" of a leader. *Leadership Quest* does a great job of helping map out this path for the future leader. It helps to breakdown some of the "fears" of wading into developing this mindset, yet is motivational to the reader to see their potential. This is a great read for any potential leader.
  - *Perry Wilhelm, CMAA, Athletic Director, Mundelein High School (IL)*

Dr. Dobbs has masterfully reminded us that leadership is influence, caring, visionary, forthright, transparent, and accountable. Good leaders chase excellence, lead change, and are relational. Our inner circle should build us up and be honest with us even when it hurts. He has reminded us that as long as the earth remains, seed time and harvest will remain...even in leadership. Dr. Dobbs has motivated me to be a better, more effective leader.
  - *Deanna (Dee) M. Stokes, Ed.S., Evangelist, Teacher, Author, and Retired Division I Basketball Coach*

Awesome! This may be Cory's best work yet. What I liked most about the fable, *Leadership Quest*, is while it is an easy read, undoubtedly every athlete that reads this book will be able to relate to the journey of leadership. This may be the best part of our summer plans right now...One Book-One Team.
  - *Tim Dougherty, Head Football Coach, Galesburg High School (IL)*

Cory has a profound way to masterfully weave storytelling and lessons on leadership. I could not put the book down. His consistent message is that leadership is a tool to be learned and mastered just like an athlete masters his or her sport. As a coaching tool or as a resource for individual pursuit of excellence in athletic leadership, this book is a must read. It helps take the scary out of those who want to be a leader but don't quite know how. This is a great leadership guide!
  - *Julie Smith, 1996 Olympic Gold Medalist, Head Softball Coach & Assistant Athletic Director, University of La Verne (CA)*

Leadership Quest by Cory Dobbs is a must read for all student-athletes and coaches. The Leadership principles discussed in the book will help anyone build a successful team!

— *Jim Johnson, Boys Basketball Coach, Greece Athena High School (NY), and Author of A Coach and a Miracle.*

"Leadership is a skill. Yes, certain people have innate qualities that can make them better at it than others, but everyone can learn how to at least recognize good, ethical leadership when they see it. It has been our privilege to work with Dr. Cory Dobbs since the inception of the Academy for Sports Leadership and watch the powerful message he delivers develop in the team setting. In *Leadership Quest* Cory has encapsulated his entire method for all to read, study, and incorporate."

— *Sam Ballard, Head Men's Basketball Coach, Mesa Community College (AZ)*

Cory Dobbs' passion for sport leadership development shines through in this quick and easy read for young emerging leaders. *Leadership Quest* follows a team manual format ideal for driving critical team discussions and nurturing the leader within us all. Dobbs writing highlights the fundamental components of successful teams and does so in a way to appeal to young aspiring sport leaders. *Leadership Quest* is full of inspirational lessons that can be used by coaches and athletes alike.

— *Cheyenne Luzynski, Ed.D Doctoral Fellow, former Alma College Coach and Administrator (MI)*

Dr. Dobbs has created a must-use tool for coaches who are building passionate, inspired leaders. Coaches should not miss this opportunity to serve their emerging leaders with this book—it is tailor-made for the student athlete.

— *Dr. Nicholas Markette, Head Coach, Hamilton High School Boy's Soccer and San Tan Soccer Club President (AZ)*

All coaches want student-athletes to step up and lead, but few take the time to show them how. Easy to read and apply, *Leadership Quest* teaches athletes important principles and helpful perspectives on their journey toward becoming dynamic, effective team leaders. An excellent resource with thought-provoking questions to help your student-athletes develop leadership skills necessary for success in both sports and life.

— *Stephanie Zonars, Coordinator of Community Outreach, Penn State University Women's Basketball, Author of Leader of the Pack and Wisdom for the Busy Coach*

Dr. Cory Dobbs leadership materials have played an integral part in opening my eyes to proper leadership development for me, our players and the Sapulpa Chieftain Football Program. His book *Leadership Quest* provides a systematic approach to building solid leaders in one's program. The phrase "we need more team leaders" is like coaches saying, "we need to be better blockers" and not providing all the proper progression and drill work associated with great blocking. Great programs have great leaders. Dr. Dobbs is the guru of teaching leadership skills! *Leadership Quest* is creatively written for those student-athletes that are serious about their future endeavors. Novice to veteran players and coaches alike will gain invaluable insight to interactive, deliberate ways to building better leaders in their programs.

— *Mike Gottsch, Head Football Coach and Asst. Athletic Director, Sapulpa High School (OK)*

As a high school coach of eleven years, I have always understood the necessity of effective leadership from my team captains and seniors. When my high expectations were not met, it was due to a lack of knowledge, not character flaws or a lack of effort. I wasn't arming my athletes with the ammunition required to become effective leaders. *Leadership Quest* provides the perfect foundation for building a leadership arsenal for athletics and for life.

    - Russ Boyer, Head Coach, Brighton High School Men's Soccer (UT)

The passion for teaching and sharing leadership concepts that develop sport leaders continues with *Leadership Quest*. I found this book packed with valuable leadership concepts and exercises that can be used when working with coaches and student athletes in leadership activities. Cory Dobbs approach remains consistent and connected to his leadership philosophy and the materials developed through the Academy for Sport Leadership.

    - Jeff Schreiner, Athletic Director, Monona Grove High School (WI)

Cory Dobbs truly "gets" leadership for today's young people, and his new book, *Leadership Quest* is an inspirational read! Cory takes old fashion values and creatively shows their importance and application in the team sport setting. The chapter leadership questions will truly inspire your athletes. I truly believe *Leadership Quest* can serve as a tool for you, as a coach, to help change the culture of your team. It is an easy, simple, entertaining read but the influence will be profound for your team.

    - Jane Albright, Women's Basketball Coach, University of Nevada at Reno

In working with the Academy for Sport Leadership, I have continued to learn more and more about leadership and how to help foster and grow leaders for my team. Cory's latest book, *Leadership Quest*: A Modern Fable for Developing the Leader Within You, will provide another great training device for my student-athletes. The story is relatable and easy to read with many great messages that my current and future leaders can use to help them on their path to great leadership.

    - Keri Sanchez, Head Coach Women's Soccer, Claremont McKenna- Harvey Mudd- Scripps Colleges (CA)

© 2012 Academy For Sport Leadership

No part of this book may be reproduced in any form without advance written permission from the publisher. No part of this publication may be stored in a retrieval system, or transmitted in any form or by any means, electronic, mechanical, photocopying, recording or otherwise, without permission of the publisher. International rights and foreign translations are available only through negotiation of a licensing agreement with the publisher.

Inquiries regarding permission for use of the material contained in this book should be addressed to:

> Premier Graphics Publishing Group
> 4141 W. Clarendon Ave.
> Phoenix, Arizona 85019
> 623.330.3831

Leadership Quest may be purchased for educational, business, or sales promotion use.

Printed in the United States of America

ISBN Number: 978-0-9839929-8-1

Leadership Quest

A MODERN DAY FABLE ON DEVELOPING THE LEADER WITHIN YOU

Cory Dobbs, Ed.D.
cory@sportleadership.com

www.sportleadership.com

Table Of Contents

The Awakening 9

Moving Forward 15

Leadership Lesson 1: Building Right Relationships 21

Leadership Lesson 2: Guiding with Influence 27

Leadership Lesson 3: Initiating Change 33

Leadership Lesson 4: Inspiring Shared Purpose 41

Leadership Lesson 5: Focusing Intentional Behavior 47

Conclusion 55

Case Studies:

Leadership Development Model 58

Case Analysis 60

The Final Push 62

The Code of Silence or a Code of Honor? 64

Winning Isn't the Only Thing 66

The Pecking Order 68

This May Hurt a Little 71

Big"We," little "me" 73

Initiating Change that Endures 75

I Didn't See the Cliff Coming... 78

Don't Rock the Boat 80

United We Stand, Divided We Can't Stand Each Other 82

Chapter 1

The Awakening

I stumbled as I got up from the desk. I'd nodded off while Mrs. Hill droned on about supply and demand. I get the idea that I'll be a better citizen and businessman if I care more about economics. Mrs. Hill is cool, but I just don't see much of a reason to stay awake when I can get some important rest prior to practice. Practice today will be brutal. We're two weeks from the end of our season. I'm glad it's almost over. It's been a terrible season. Our 7 – 17 record tells only half the story.

Traveling at a brisk pace through the hallway I'm hoping to run into Taylor. I haven't seen her yet today and want to wish her well in her game tonight. Taylor is one of my best friends. I've known her since 8th grade and have relied on her to help me handle some of the tough times I've gone through the past couple of years. My parents divorce. My brother's addiction and never-ending rehab. She's not my girlfriend, though I think she'd be jealous if I told her about my interest in Jessica Snyder. But that's for another day.

I can't wait to drop my bomb on Taylor. Saturday night I stayed home, just wanting to chill. I didn't like the selection of pay-per-view movies—and anyway my mom makes me pay for those movies with chores. Not an option. Reading the descriptions of the movies on the movie channels I came across a story about a high school wrestler who has underachieved for three years and decides he's going to do something about it. That'll work, I thought to myself. I can relate. As of today, I'm not sure my high school basketball legacy is going to be all that meaningful or inspiring. I poured myself a Monster and dumped a bag of Doritos onto a paper plate. I Googled the movie, *Vision Quest*, to see if I knew any of the actors in this old-school flick. None.

    The movie really got to me. This guy, Louden Swain, is entering his senior year and realizes he's wasted his time because he hasn't challenged himself athletically. So he decides to make his mark by moving into a different weight class and take on the best wrestler in the state. He reveals this unthinkable goal to his best friend who calls it a "Vision Quest." A vision quest, his friend tells him, is a Native American rite of passage. It takes place when a young person envisions a turning point in their life and from that moment forward their quest is to chase after their vision. Well, by the end of the movie I too had a vision quest. Mine is to become a dynamic team leader helping lead our team out of mediocrity. A Leadership Quest if you will.

    Coach Sparks has always told me I could be a leader. I'm not really sure what he wants me to do when he says this, but I do know that we've not had any team leaders in the past few years. Seems it might be a pretty important role. And my dad, the CEO of Donahue Tires, is always on me for not being a leader. I guess it's his way of trying to get me to be a leader. Anyway, I want to fulfill my promise as a leader and pursue my Leadership Quest to become the best team leader in the state. I know that my first step is taking ownership of the process of learning to lead. Funny thing is, in order to do this I feel like I need to follow Taylor. She's always been a leader. People enjoy following her and she has a mindset for leadership. I've grown tired of playing on mediocre teams and I'm thinking my leadership might be an answer to our problems. Taylor's teams seem to always win.

I didn't see Taylor in the hall so I'm running to my Government class or I'll be late for the second time in three days. I'll let Mr. Mays know I've gotta go to the restroom and I'll text her.

I wasn't quite sure what to make of a comment Coach Sparks made to me in practice today. He told me I need to stretch myself, to leave my cocoon of comfort and find my way into "the school of hard knocks." I think he's sensing what I'm feeling. I need to really change my mindset and learn how to fulfill my leadership potential. I'm looking forward to sharing my Leadership Quest with Taylor.

After practice I ran into her in the school courtyard. "Thanks for the text," Taylor said. "I know you've got something on your mind. Can it hold for a few more minutes?" she requested. I told her it could.

"OK. Come with me to Mr. Carter's classroom. I forgot a book I'm reading in his room. He usually leaves around 5:30 so let's run." She's always moving at a fast pace.

Mr. Carter is a popular English teacher and he's respected by most students. Carter was a former officer in the Army. I'm not sure what level, but he served in Iraq about ten years ago. He is, as he tells us, battle-tested and ready for anything. I don't think any student has ever really tried to get under his skin. He's always calm. I think everyone senses he's always in control of himself and the situation. For my money he is one of the best leaders in our school.

Taylor opened the door to Mr. Carter's room. He wasn't around so we walked in and she plucked her book off his desk. The book she's reading is called *The Leadership Challenge*. It figures. "You reading that?" I asked. "I'm studying every word," she said. It figures.

We turned to leave just as Mr. Carter walked through the door. "Hey Taylor," said Carter. "I knew you'd come by to get your book. Left it on my desk." Turns out Carter read the book years ago. He's a West Pointer and enjoys reading leadership stuff.

"Mr. Carter, this is my friend Drew," chirped Taylor. "I think he's going to be a great leader," she continued. What! How in the world does she know? Is she psychic and somehow knows my Leadership Quest before I reveal it to her?

Taylor asked Mr. Carter what he thought was the most important thing he learned from his leadership experience in the military. Without blinking Carter passionately explained, "I learned there is no good leadership without good character. A close second is the life lesson that I learned at the Academy—that leadership development is a lifelong commitment. It's a never-ending process of seeking excellence in one's self and those one associates with."

Taylor shot me a look. "Good stuff. Mr. Carter is a leader that I'm learning lots from. You may not know this Drew," she grinned, "I expect to be a leader in whatever I do. Mr. Carter is mentoring me, teaching me about living up to my highest standards with courage. I'm learning about self-discipline, integrity, success, motivation, and teamwork."

"Have you ever thought about being a leader?" Mr. Carter asked me. I didn't feel comfortable telling him about my Leadership Quest, but I answered, "Yes. I'm looking forward to it someday."

I was reluctant to go further into a conversation with the two well-schooled leaders, but I found the courage and asked him a question. "Mr. Carter, what is the number one thing I can do as a leader to bring my team together?" Without any hesitation he replied, "Believe in them, and let them know you believe in them. Help each teammate to believe in himself. Or herself," he said nodding at Taylor. "Help your teammates to believe in each other. Help them to see their potentials—and not just on the playing field—how their potential is multiplied when everyone on the team cares about the team's performance rather than just their own performance."

Mr. Carter reached for a bundle of used popsicle sticks on his desk. He handed the bundle to me. "Go ahead, try to break this bundle." I took one attempt and failed. I looked at Taylor and said, "You wanna shot at this superstar?" Taylor, as she so often does, anticipated Mr. Carter's point. She took some scissors out of a basket on the desk, cut the cord around the bundle of sticks and snapped one in half. She laughed and said, "Mr. Carter taught me this lesson last week."

"Individually, just about anything or anyone can be broken," Mr. Carter explained. "But together, this bundle of sticks can't be broken. Think of your team. What seems to be an impossible task becomes very possible when you believe in each other and work together. Your number one challenge is getting your teammates to truly believe this in their hearts and minds."

Chapter 2

Moving Forward

It's Friday. Game day. Playing Edison High School tonight. We're out of the playoffs and they're on the bubble—on the edge and I expect they'll play that way. I know they're gonna go all out in an effort to secure the last playoff spot. Our practices this week were just okay. I wonder if it's part of the human condition to lose motivation to win when the game has little meaning.

Taylor texted me wishing our team well. She's never really wished me luck, always the team. I wonder if this is part of her leadership mindset.

Something struck me as I was driving to the gym. When Mr. Carter asked if I wanted to be a leader I reflexively responded with *someday* I'd like to be a leader. Funny how that's what came out when I was caught off guard. My habit with school work is to procrastinate until the last minute, then whip something together and hope for the best. Is that what a high impact team leader does?

I walked around the locker room talking to my teammates. I wished everyone a good game. But Dan Hutchings, our starting center, growled and shook his head side-to-side to say "no" as I approached him. Why was Dan shaking me off? I took another step toward him. He turned and walked in the other direction.

Dan is a likeable guy. I've known him since our freshman year. I'm guessing he too is tired of the mediocrity we've been anchored in for three years. Maybe he's just had enough of the usual routine of players telling other players to have a good game, yet doing little to bring out the best in each other during practice. At that moment I recognized that unrealized potential turns into a hollow pain. I hope to talk to Dan about this sometime soon.

We lost. Edison beat us by twenty points. I wonder if apathy is like a virus. One player has it and spreads it to the others.

Saturday began with my mother making pancakes. Good stuff. I texted Taylor to see if she had time to meet with me today. I couldn't wait any longer to tell her about my Leadership Quest. She asked me to meet her at Starbucks.

"Morning Drew," Taylor nodded as I approached her table. "Hi Taylor, I'm glad you've got time for me," I said kiddingly. Taylor always has time for me. She is that one individual I can always count on. After witnessing our apathetic performance in last night's game and having Dan Hutchings ignore me puts into perspective the kind of teammate Taylor is—a sincere and genuine one.

"Okay, I'm not really going to build up to what I need to tell you," I said. I was excited and couldn't wait any longer. "So, here goes. Saturday night I watched this really inspiring movie. It hit me so deeply that before it was over I had a vision for a future I want to make happen. The lead character in the movie is a lot like me, complacent and satisfied with underachieving.

And then he has this burst of insight that his life will change if he takes on and beats the best wrestler in the state. I know, I left out the detail that the guy's an average wrestler who, like me, has had little athletic success. But one day he suddenly has what his best friend calls a Vision Quest. In fact, that's the name of the movie."

Taylor took a long sip from her vanilla latte and studied my face. She burst out laughing. "Vision Quest? I know the movie. The soundtrack has some Madonna songs. Love it," she smirked. "I have the DVD. I watch it once a year to remind me of the power of belief in one's self and the energy that emerges from a clear vision." Taylor surprised me. An old-school motivational movie and she owns it? It figures.

Taylor reached into her book bag and pulled out a notebook. "Drew, let me share my notes on this movie and my Vision Quest with you." "Okay," I said, but didn't we meet here so I could share my Vision Quest with you?" Taylor smiled and shot me a wink. "I'm sorry, please share with me your thoughts and ideas, what you took away from this emotionally charged, life-changing movie," she offered lightheartedly.

For the next fifteen minutes I talked and she listened. I explained how this simple movie resonated with me, striking to my core. How it triggered in me a moment in my life when I knew that I had to change. To grow. Finally, I gifted her a moment to share her thoughts about my Leadership Quest.

She reached for her notebook and pulled out some well-worn notes. In an excited voice Taylor said, "One of the things I learned from the movie is that success is created through the performance of a few small deliberate habits. Disciplined routines if you will, that build up over time to produce results far beyond anything you might expect. The reality is that little successes are easy to achieve each day, but you have to be deliberate. And those little successes lead to big successes!"

Taylor paused for moment, taking a sip from her latte. She glanced at me. My mouth was shut so she continued. "It's like the farmer. The farmer begins each day with a game plan. Plow the dirt. Fertilize the soil. Plant the seeds. Water the crops. Days come and days go. Little happens. The farmer maintains his patience and trusts that this process will yield crops. And it does! The care, nurturing, and cultivation that for some time yields little, eventually produces a harvest. There are no shortcuts."

Taylor continued, "As team leaders we need to develop trust and patience for the team building process like the farmer has for growing his crops. Remember when Mr. Carter told us that we need to guide our team's belief in teamwork, it's the same process."

"You and I can lead our teammates to believe in each other by constantly working with them to become mentally strong and physically tough. Finding ways to practice team unity. We can't simply come together on game night and expect it to happen. It's nurtured and cultivated in practice, in weekend get-togethers, in the way we build relationships on a daily basis. When we do the right things the right way, all our small choices and behaviors accumulate. And then one day, seemingly out of nowhere, everything comes together and the team becomes the center of everyone's experience."

Taylor made me an offer. "We all need good role

models if we are to become good leaders. I've been blessed to have a handful of role models in my life. Drew, if you're ready to move forward with your Leadership Quest let me know. I'd like to help you develop the leader within you.

Since taking on my Leadership Quest I've met some great leaders and learned how to make leadership a major force in my life. Discipline is needed in planning and carrying out your new personal vision. You've got to dig deep within yourself, relentlessly looking for ways to pull it out."

Taylor slowed her pace. "Learning to lead requires entering into uncharted waters. And in order to get where you don't know you can go, you'll have to be willing to take risks and make mistakes. Learning leadership requires accepting that failing is part of the learning process. The learning process will include some false starts, some mistakes. Mistakes are great teachers, but to learn from them you need to shift your thinking to a leadership mindset."

Chapter 3

Leadership Lesson 1: Building Right Relationships

Our last game ended quickly. Morrison High jumped out to a 20 – 6 lead and never looked back. Wish I didn't have to look back. But I have to learn to be reflective. Taylor instructed me that leadership is as much an intellectual adventure as it is an emotional journey. She says hands-on experience is usually the best teacher. But discovering what it takes to create excellence requires team leaders—of which I now want to be one more than anything—to learn to look backward and learn from experience.

Ever since I told Taylor about my Leadership Quest she's been calling me, texting me, and pushing me to devote time to learning everything I can about leadership. Talk about relentless. I'm guessing one day Taylor will be known by millions because she is determined to impact the lives of others.

My cell phone rang, it was Taylor. "Drew, ya ready?" I forgot we had an appointment today with Mrs. Robin Collins. Mrs. Collins coached softball at three NCAA Division One schools, winning two national championships. She also coached at the high school level and won a state championship. Taylor arranged for us to meet with her to learn some strategies for becoming a team leader. She told me she meets with her twice a year. With Mr. Carter as a mentor and Coach Collins as a personal teacher it's becoming clear to me why Taylor excels at leadership.

Coach Collins' office was in the Donnithorne building on the campus of the university. Even though she'd retired four years ago she still had an office in the athletic complex.

Using a White Board we broke the team building process down into eight "impact areas" with Coach Collins pointing out to us the importance of each area. She said an impact area is any part of the team building process that has a direct impact on the team's results and the development of the players. We identified offensive skill, offensive strategy, defensive skill, defensive strategy, health and physical conditioning, mental toughness, practice management, and team cohesion as impact areas that met her bottom line criteria.

"Now," Coach Collins began, "as a team captain—I like the term *team leader* better—which impact area can you have the greatest effect on?" Taylor held back, obviously to give me the opportunity to respond. I quickly said, "team cohesion."

"Yes," Coach Collins confirmed. "Team cohesion is simply the interpersonal bonds that hold a team together. Now, how you build and strengthen those bonds is what causes coaches headaches." She added, "Players that create cohesive teams are more likely to accept the team's vision and goals, coaching decisions, and cultivate positive norms. And when stronger bonds are created through healthy interpersonal interactions, the invisible connections become visible showing up in the won-loss column. More wins. But more importantly a cohesive team creates a positive environment that makes for a better learning experience for everyone."

Taylor asked, "So, what should we be doing to strengthen bonds between teammates? Don't you just like someone or not?" I knew Taylor wouldn't be quiet for long. Like I said, she's relentless. I want to be relentless too.

"Let me explain," nodded Coach Collins. "It's not so much as liking, though that helps, it's more about building what I call right relationships. A right relationship is one in which individuals find the right way to interact with one another. That is, Taylor you and I have one way of relating to each other and Drew and I may develop a different way of relating. Every relationship is customized. That's what makes it tricky," grinned Coach Collins.

Coach Collins continued, "But what makes a relationship so powerful is when it is built on two immutable principles. These two principles must always be present in order to create a right relationship. The first principle is taken from the proverb that teaches us that as iron sharpens iron, so one person sharpens another. That is, when we sharpen something, we improve it. You see, the easiest person to lie to, to let down, is ourselves. We are great defenders of our actions. We can always find an excuse to explain away our shortcomings or misdeeds. But if we have teammates that hold us responsible for what we do and accountable to one another we can eliminate excuses. Let me just say this, it works."

Coach Collins then shared with us a scenario that demonstrates the importance of building right relationships. "The coach walks to the mound to visit with the pitcher and the catcher. An emotionally charged pitcher in the heat of battle is usually not the player most likely to acknowledge reality. The catcher is. When the coach asks the catcher 'How's the pitcher doing?,' the catcher is expected to tell the coach the truth. If the catcher is fearful of telling the coach the truth, fearing her teammate may disagree with her and hold it against her, the team will pay a price."

She continued, "Too often we buy into the lie that making peace is better than telling the truth. We do this mistakenly as an effort to solve a problem without ever addressing the real issue. The point is, great teams need strong leaders capable of telling the hard truth *and receiving the hard truth*. That's how you build right relationships!"

Taylor's head bobbed up and down. "Mr. Carter," She said in a giddy tone, "told us that the fundamental guiding principle that drives relationships, the way of life, at West Point is that a cadet will not lie, cheat, or steal." She paused, *"nor tolerate those that do!* Wow, how powerful it must be to have that kind of relationship with your teammates. Living life to be the best you can be takes teamwork. I think I'll apply to West Point!"

Coach Collins finished her point. "The second principle of building right relationships is that the deeper your relationships, the stronger your leadership. To gain the commitment of your teammates you've got to work hard to deepen relationships. And it's not just the positive things that deepen a relationship. Relationships will invariably include disagreements, disappointments, setbacks, and conflict. What matters is how each individual responds to and resolves these matters."

Coach Collins in a low raspy whisper concluded,

"The best teams don't simply work on their sport skills and strategy. They get into each other's lives. We are family, for better or for worse, and we need to connect with each other. Team life is about building strong, caring, trust-based, long-term relationships." I could tell by her shift to "we" that, for her, these two powerful principles necessary for building right relationships are integrated into who she is and what she does.

I really enjoyed learning from Coach Collins. I'm glad Taylor is my friend, one that's concerned about who I am and what I do. I'm getting the point that leadership is about relationships, human connections. I now know that my teammates are enriched in terms of what they can accomplish through the quality of relationships they develop with each other. In the past it's been pretty easy to sacrifice relationships. I've never been really close to any of my teammates. I've never had that deep relationship with others that Coach Collins is talking about. I plan to make building right relationships a priority in my life, especially with my teammates.

Leadership Development Exercises

Leading Self
- How do you respond when you're in a situation where you want to tell the truth, but you know that telling the truth will cause tension in your life?

Leading Others
- Your beliefs guide the way you behave. How do Taylor's beliefs differ from Drew's? What are the results of Drew's beliefs? Taylor's beliefs?

Leading with Others

As a team discuss the following questions regarding the disease of excuse-making.
- What are some ways student-athletes find excuses to:
    - put forth only as much energy as is needed to participate
    - not be accountable for their actions
    - not hold themselves responsible to teammates
    - not commit to teammates

Leadership Actions that Lead to Building Right Relationships

- Hold teammates to higher standards
- Confront controversy and conflict
- Provide honest feedback
- Listen attentively to teammates
- Always treat everyone with dignity and respect
- Show trust and speak the truth
- Look for and compliment the good in others
- Use the force of constructive criticism
- Help teammates meet their needs and achieve their goals
- Don't gossip
- Allow your teammates to make mistakes
- Be a positive person to be around

Chapter 4

Leadership Lesson 2: Guiding with Influence

My father says that if you treat people like gold, they'll shine like gold. As the top leader in his company he always puts others first. I remember reading an article written about him in the business newspaper that said he's a successful leader because he makes it possible for people to flourish and grow. In the article he said, "To be a trustworthy leader you need to care about the lives of the people you lead. People willingly follow a person of integrity. And more often than not people quit people, before they quit companies."
I know I've quit on my teammates before. And it's obvious that as a team we've all quit on each other. Totally a reciprocal thing—you quit on me and I'll quit on you.

Funny how I now understand and relate to what my dad said. In the past I used to take in what he would say with one ear and let it roll out the other. I'm changing that mindset.

I'm having lunch with him today and I want to tell him about my Leadership Quest. Maybe not everything. Just enough to see what he has to say.

I called Dan Hutchings yesterday. I haven't heard back from him. Right after our final game of the season

I committed to my quest to be the best team leader I can become. And spending time with Dan is on my list of things to do.

Waiting for my dad to pick me up I opened *The Leadership Moment*, a book Taylor got for me. My goal is a chapter a day, though I read the first two yesterday. I plunged into chapter 3 and was half-way through when I had to stop. The words on the page slammed into me.

Optimism is a collective construction, a shared view of the world based on a complex blend of what is and what ought to be.

For three years now our team has been without optimism. Coach Sparks isn't a negative coach. In fact he's very positive in most of the things he does. However, my teammates and I have simply turned a blind eye to the subtle but negative cumulative effects of our poor relationships and our lack of perseverance in the face of obstacles. But there it was, *Optimism is a collective construction*. That means it's something we as a team need to build—construct if you will. And if it's something we build we're gonna need tools.

As we drove over the river I wondered how I would begin a leadership conversation with my dad. He always puts me first, but I'm not sure where I put him. The divorce thing kinda turned me against him in some ways. Ways I chose not to explore. Rather, I numb myself with my IPod when those thoughts arise. Facing reality means dealing with things I'd prefer to avoid. Leaders, Taylor says, face reality as it is, not as it was or as you wish it were. Taylor is a lighthouse guiding me through the rough waters of becoming a leader.

I know I'll have to confront those negative feelings in order to grow as a person and to become an effective leader. Coach Collins voice is ringing in my mind "We are a family, and for better or worse, we need to connect." Yes, I'm gonna connect with my dad and my teammates.

"Dad," I started, "we finished our season 7 – 21. That's 21 losses! I know that winning isn't everything. That people sometimes sacrifice too much simply to win something with little lasting value. But I want to be on a winning team next year and I want the experience to be something I can build on. I know that I need to be a leader and I've begun working on it."

I asked my dad if leadership can be learned. "Becoming a leader isn't easy," he said excitedly. "Just as becoming a doctor or lawyer is not easy, leadership isn't either. Becoming a leader requires a solid leadership education. Learning to lead may seem easier for some, those gifted with the right opportunities, but the process of becoming a leader requires developing a leadership mindset and skill set. And these things anyone can learn if they put in the time to learn and seek out leadership opportunities. He concluded his opening statement by asserting "Leadership is about people—about trust."

He then told me a few things about building commitment and making the most of everyone's talents. "If you desire to be an effective leader," my dad said with a hint of a lecture in his voice, "you'll succeed by being a person of influence. You see Drew, in my business I have power and authority—the power to hire and fire and the authority to say yes or no. But in a peer leadership situation your best leadership strategy is influence. You've got to find ways to influence and impact the hearts and minds of your teammates."

I was truly present with my father. I wasn't simply

nodding to make him think I was listening. I was listening. And learning!

"So dad," I cheerfully asked, "how do I influence my teammates?"

My dad eagerly responded. "Your teammates will be influenced by what they see. If you want to influence them, be a role model. Align what you say with what you do. Be noticed as someone who is trustworthy. They expect you to do what you say you will do. Serve as a guide helping them identify where they want to go and then guiding them there. Walking alongside them. Actively support your teammates. Encourage them. Build their confidence and communicate with them on an emotional level—that's influencing the heart. Leadership starts in the heart."

My dad sure was glad to share his insights and experience with me. He continued, "Once you've touched the hearts of your teammates you can then influence their minds. You do this by helping your teammates set a course and direction by acknowledging their goals and ambitions. And finding ways to help your teammates understand how values influence behavior and how our attitudes and behaviors affect others."

He smiled and said, "When you can influence the head and the heart you can unleash the energy and emotion within a person," concluding his message with force. It sounds so simple. I now know I'll need to learn how to influence the hearts and minds of my teammates. I'm up for the challenge.

I had one other item on my learning agenda for my dad. "Dad, something hit me today while I was waiting for you. I'm reading a book that my friend Taylor gave to me. The writer is a professor of leadership at one of the premier universities on the East Coast, not sure which one. Anyway, he says that optimism is a collective construction. If it's something we can construct, what kinds of tools do I need?" I waited as he collected his thoughts.

My dad looked at me and said, "Drew, leadership in a team environment requires you to painstakingly find answers to three fundamental questions. One, do you know how to bring out the best in every teammate? Two, do you know how to capture the hearts and minds of your teammates. And three, do you know what destroys a relationship?" I could barely keep up with him. These questions caused a buzz in my mind. No, a blur.

Leadership Development Exercises

Leading Self
- It's likely you've broken a promise or commitment you've made to another teammate. What steps can you take to restore the relationship?

Leading Others
- Do you see yourself as an influencer? If so, why? If not, how can you expand your self-image to see yourself as an influencer?

Leading with Others
- In the last paragraph above, Drew's dad gave him some tools to guide him in constructing team optimism. The tools are the questions he left him with. Spend some time thinking through these questions with your teammates. Have each team member describe "This is how to bring out the best in me." Take notes.

Leadership Actions that Lead to Guiding with Influence

- Model desired actions and attitudes
- Encourage others to develop an achievement mindset
- Demonstrate persistence and resilience
- Make actions consistent with words
- Willingly make sacrifices
- Promote higher levels of involvement
- Think and act confidently
- Become more likable

Chapter 5

Leadership Lesson 3: Initiating Change

    Taylor honked the horn of her black Honda Civic. I grabbed my leadership notebook off the bed and rushed out the door. "Did you remember your notebook," Taylor said in a low voice, her eyes darting to her thick and over-flowing notebook in the passenger's seat. She is relentless.

    I got in the car and rolled up the sleeves to my new shirt. Taylor has gotten me in the habit of rolling my sleeves up two inches above my wrists. She says it's a symbolic gesture to an old-school practice of "rolling up your sleeves" signifying you're ready for work. I really think she's got me doing it as a fashion trend. She'd probably have me stop doing it if I told her that Jessica Snyder likes it.

    As Taylor and I drove up to a red brick apartment building, I expressed my thanks to her for helping me along my journey. I am quickly discovering the meaning of leadership and learning the practices that will help me succeed as a team leader. Taylor says that the most important part of my being a leader is to create more leaders. I'm sure that's why she's taken me under her wings.

    I'm a few weeks into my Leadership Quest and I

now know that a leadership foundation is built on self-leadership. I've got to lead myself before others will follow. If you can't lead yourself, you'll never be able to lead your teammates. And once you become skilled at leading yourself you move to leading others and then the final level of leadership—leading *with* others. These are some new ideas I have about leadership, the result of the inspirational teaching of my mentor Taylor.

As we made our way to our destination I asked innocently, "Where we going?" Taylor corrected me, "Where *are* we going?" Relentless.

Taylor said with a petite smile, "Terrell Davis plays for a D-3 school somewhere in the Midwest. He's home for the summer. He's a leader I met through Coach Collins. Coach Collins recommended I seek out Terrell and find out from a student-athlete some keys to peer leadership. Coach Collins said that Terrell is one of the finest team leaders in America."

So I now had an answer to my question Where are we going. In our time together over the past few weeks, Taylor has had an exceptionally strong influence on me. She's helping me to lean into change, embracing the dynamic challenges of taking my dormant leadership skills to a higher level. She has me holding myself to higher standards and living life with a sense of urgency.

As we approached the door I could hear Bruno Mars playing in the background. I'm looking forward to meeting Terrell. "Hey Drew, where's your leadership notebook? Get it," Taylor paused. "You're gonna need it," she said as she threw me the keys to her car.

Terrell lived with his older brother during the summer. The apartment was nice, but not much bigger than my living room at home. "Why do you want to be a team leader," Terrell asked. I gave him the shallow standard answer all kids give, but I included that I was tired of being a complacent student and an average athlete playing on mediocre teams.

"Wake up every morning and be all about excellence," Terrell instructed. "Develop a change mindset. So making today better than yesterday is the way you think. Always remember that if you're not chasing excellence and change, mediocrity is all you'll get. You should wake up every morning with a mindset ready to pursue the success driving question *What can I improve today?* That way you wake up and you're committed to making this day better than yesterday," Terrell explained.

Terrell is passionately committed to world-class leadership and dedicated to his teammates. He brings to his team the perfect combination of competitive drive and a profound desire to make sure everyone on his team can win together. With a get-up-and-go tone to his voice, he continued, "We can't just respond to change, we have to lead change. We have to focus on actually getting things done. Inspiring our teammates to be their very best. Change is about learning and inspiring others to come along with you."

One word came to my mind, relentless. It is obvious that Terrell, like Taylor, Coach Collins, and Mr. Carter, is relentless. Okay, I'm committing to being relentless.

In an effort to jump-start my new relentless attitude I asked, "So, Terrell, have you always been a leader?" In the short time I've been chasing my vision to become a team leader I've encountered the philosophical question of whether a leader is born or made. Some coaches promote leadership as something a player either has or doesn't have, while other coaches believe that all students have leadership potential. "Drew," Terrell began, "I thought I was a born leader when I was in high school because my coaches asked me, not the other players, to step up and lead. I assumed that because coaches were asking me to lead, it meant that I was a born leader. That all I had to do was be myself. Was I wrong! The more I learn and experience leadership it is clear that leadership can be learned and that no one is born with a leadership gene."

I was feeling confident after asking the first question, so I relentlessly asked another, "What is your role as a team leader? Terrell jumped on this one too. "Your primary role as a team leader is to mobilize your teammates, to get them beyond the edge of familiar terrain. When you get your teammates into unfamiliar terrain, going beyond self-imposed boundaries, new learning and new behaviors take place. Often, deeply held perceptions need to be changed. For example, the perception that I was a born leader simply held me captive in a pattern of status quo. But when I changed my belief to view leaders as being made, well let's just say it was at that point in my life where I began to find ways to grow and develop as a leader. You see, change usually requires loss," Terrell said leaning forward.

He pulled out from under the coffee table a large white notebook. He quickly turned to a page filled with diagrams. I thought this must be his playbook. It wasn't. It was his leadership notebook. He vanished for a minute into his bedroom. He returned wheeling out his own White Board. Great leaders are serious aren't they?

He wrote on the board,

Goal	Give Up
1. _____	1. _____
2. _____	2. _____
3. _____	3. _____
4. _____	4. _____

Terrell walked over and put his hand on my shoulder. "Drew, put this in your notebook," he suggested. Waving the marker in the air he began instructing. "This is the first principle of change that you'll want to share with your teammates. Write down four goals you want to achieve and next to each goal write down what you will have to give up, sacrifice, or risk in order to achieve the goal."

Taylor, having already copied the contents on the board in her notebook added, "It's like the caterpillar. It has to give up its legs in order to fly. The fundamental way of life for the caterpillar changes during its metamorphosis." "Great example," Terrell said commandingly. Adding, "You have to take risks in order to change."

"When you and your teammates make a purposeful, consistent, and relentless effort to change you'll unleash untapped potential," he said. Thumbing through his notebook Terrell began humming to himself. "You can profoundly improve your team if everyone commits one hour a week to team building training. You and your teammates working together to build on each other's contributions and perspectives, setting and raising performance standards, and building confidence in one another" he added.

He found the page he was looking for. Grabbing his

marker he spun around and using a napkin wiped the White Board clean. He wrote **Deliberate Practice** in black bold letters on the board. Reaching into his back pocket he pulled out a red marker. Below *Deliberate Practice* he jotted, *Group Discussions, Role Play, Case Studies.*

"These are just three ways you and your teammates can practice becoming a better team outside of the practice and game setting. This kind of practice is necessary for change—the metamorphosing process if you will. We use resources we get from The Academy for Sport Leadership to guide our group discussions, learning conversations, and case studies," said Terrell.

Without drawing a breath he continued, "As a team, usually without the coaches, we gather for an hour every Tuesday and talk. We spend time connecting. We discuss such things as team culture. We've created a scorecard to help us understand where we are in the process of building a culture of trust. We do case studies that fundamentally change the way we work together. These exercises and activities encourage us to ask each other tough questions, to share our insights, and promote participation. We often end up laughing at ourselves.

By talking together we gain insight into our fears, frustrations, and failures. Together we tackle some of the harder issues like relationships and conflict, disagreements and disappointments. The point is, we don't want to be making up solutions in a crisis, when a problem emerges, during a setback, or when adversity comes our way. We want to know what to do."

It seems like it's been a year since I started my Leadership Quest. I've changed, and I'm changing. I've learned that no matter how much desire you have and how much knowledge you've gained, no change will be successful unless you expend the effort necessary to bring it about. If you spend your life clinging to what is comfortable and secure, you'll likely attain little. When you stay in that cocoon of comfort that Coach Sparks talks about, you risk numbing yourself to the status quo—depriving your heart and mind of the joy of meaningful achievement.

Leadership Development Exercises

Leading Self
- Learning involves change. Learning is the act or process by which behavioral change, habits, knowledge, skills and attitudes are acquired. List some habits you want to change. Use these four categories to list habits for change: Physical, Intellectual, Emotional, and Social.

Leading Others
- Write down a few fears you have about leading your teammates. What steps can you take to eliminate those fears?

Leading with Others
- With your teammates, explore the barriers to change. What physical, intellectual, emotional, and social barriers exist that are likely to challenge your team to maximize its potential? List at least three barriers for each category. Once you've finished with the barriers to change, identify actions steps to overcome the barriers to change.

Leadership Actions that Lead to Initiating Change

- Make action a habit, always take the first step
- Stop doing unproductive things
- Make change meaningful
- Feed the need of teammates to learn and grow
- Build your teammates confidence and destroy their fears
- Cultivate positive attitude towards change
- Take the initiative in building friendships
- Foster dissatisfaction with the status quo
- Be intentional, find or create experiences to learn from
- Make reflection a daily learning habit

Chapter 6

Leadership Lesson 4: Inspiring Shared Purpose

Hip-hop blared through my car as I drove past sky scrapers pointing toward the heavens. After an exhausting day yesterday I needed the music to wake me up. My excitement has been building since last night. Taylor has done it again. She has arranged for us to meet another dynamic leader. She won't tell me who it is, and she won't tell me where we're goin. "Turn left at the light," Taylor grinned. "I'll pay for parking," she said.

The history lecture hall was a very large fan-shaped auditorium. The professor, a middle-aged fellow, according to Taylor is well-educated and well-liked by the students and the community. We slid into a couple of seats in the back row.

The professor was discussing the Bay of Pigs incident. I recall hearing about it in one of my history classes, but nothing is registering. "How can leaders foster more effective connecting of the dots within organizations?," bellowed the professor. "Leaders can work on their facilitation skills," he said answering his own question. He continued, "And they can alter approaches in various group settings. They can manage air time—ensuring that a few people do not dominate the discussion." I'm lost. I'm not really following him. Actually, I probably can't follow him because I don't know what he's talking about. I hope this isn't the "lesson" Taylor brought me here to learn.

Taylor scheduled an appointment for us to meet with Dr. Troy Knight. "Does his name ring a bell?," she asked me as we departed the auditorium and made our way to the professor's office. "Not at all. Should it?" I asked shaking my head.

Taylor explained to me that Dr. Knight was a former football player. He played for the Green Bay Packers in the 1990's and was a vital cog in turning the team from a perennial loser into a winning organization. Troy Knight was a back-up tight-end, she told me. Yet he was their best team leader. He played eight seasons with the Packers before a knee injury forced him to retire. When he retired he chose to pursue his dream of being a college professor.

"Good afternoon, Dr. Knight, I'm Taylor Roberts. And this is my friend Drew Donahue. We are excited to be here. We're student-athletes in search of excellence," Taylor said smiling, standing firm while shaking his hand. "I would have preferred to sit in the front seats today, but since we didn't pay for the class it wasn't appropriate to take a seat that belongs to a paying student," Taylor said with authority. Relentless. She's absolutely relentless.

"Another front-seater. I too am a front-seater," said Dr. Knight with a gleam. "Yes, sir," Taylor said, clearly owning the practice of sitting in the front row. "If I sit in the back I'm with people only half serious about the topic or course. When I sit in the front I'm surrounded by people interested in success and achievement," Taylor beamed. I'm sitting in the front from now on.

Leadership Lesson 4: Inspiring Shared Purpose

Taylor began to interview Dr. Knight. She asked him about his high school and college experiences as a student-athlete. She probed for leadership lessons. After about ten minutes Dr. Knight offered us some water. He left the room and returned with two bottles and a notebook. It was obvious to me, this was his leadership notebook. Seems the best leaders have one.

Dr. Knight opened his leadership notebook to a quote. He read, *"The quality of a person's life is in direct proportion to their commitment to excellence, regardless of their chosen field of endeavor."* He paused, gathered his voice and said, "My playing career, from high school to the pros was a journey. I played on some teams that were good, some great. I preferred the great. But great teams didn't always win. You see, I learned a long time ago that when I—and my teammates—commit to something together, we have an opportunity to really learn, grow, develop, and enjoy the experience. When that sense of a collective commitment was missing the trivial issues always wasted far too much of our energy to enjoy the experience let alone win games. By the way, that quote is from Vince Lombardi. An important figure in leadership and excellence, not just football."

Knight continued, "Our championship season, and interestingly our worst season—record wise—were the two most enjoyable years I played for the Packers. Both seasons the players enjoyed working together and were united in purpose, which lead to extraordinarily high morale. Both teams, one winning the other losing, had commitment to a shared purpose. Our shared purpose defined what we should do to pursue our collective aspirations. And just as importantly it clarified for us what not to do if we wanted to get to our desired destination. In life, we are all looking for something that gives meaning and direction to our lives. A purpose. Don't get me wrong, while winning a championship is certainly nice, there are many other worthy purposes that can give equal, if not more, meaning to life."

Staring at the two of us Dr. Knight elaborated, "Over the years I've discovered that challenging teammates to a serious commitment only works when a purpose has been defined and the players are in alignment mentally and emotionally. During our championship season, everyone on the team knew we were capable of winning it all. What gave meaning to us that season was the pursuit of excellence as measured by a championship. At the time we were comfortable that all the energy and effort we'd invested over the previous three seasons was to bear fruit for this one season—an opportunity to validate our commitment to excellence."

Dr. Knight pushed his chair back and raised his voice, "*Aaannnddd* the year that we had a losing season, but a ton of fun, we were in a rebuilding mode and our purpose each day was to learn how to overcome adversity and setbacks. We knew that we had to grow individually and develop our unity, so our purpose was simply to focus on getting better every day. Our coaching staff had the vision to see opportunities within our circumstances. We didn't measure our success by wins and losses, by how other teams in our division were doing. Rather, we measured our success by the improvements we made each day. Jot this down in your notebook: *A clear and compelling purpose is necessary to build an atmosphere of optimism*. We were losing games yet we came to work each day with a strong sense of purpose and optimism."

"By the way," Dr. Knight lingered, "the championship team came two years after our worst season. Our championship season wouldn't have been possible without us sowing the seeds of excellence in our losing season, allowing us to eventually reap a Super Bowl victory." Dr. Knight drilled his final point, "You reap what you sow. Always!"

On the way home I asked Taylor to drive. I want to review my notes. Wow! Am I becoming relentless?

Leadership Development Exercises

Leading Self
- What is your vision for your upcoming season? What values are involved in your vision?

Leading Others
- How will you deal with a "toxic" teammate, one that doesn't care much about the team's vision?

Leading with Others
- Hold a discussion with your teammates to identify your collective aspirations. Discuss how each individual's values might help or hinder the team's shared purpose.

Leadership Actions that Lead to Inspiring Shared Purpose

- Generate passion and pride in team's vision
- Heighten commitment to purpose and goals
- Foster a strong team attitude
- Communicate a need to be connected to something larger than ourselves
- Celebrate contributions of teammates
- Cultivate ownership over rentership

Chapter 7

Leadership Lesson 5: Focusing Intentional Behavior

In reviewing my notes from our meeting with Dr. Knight I learned that we live at a time when change is taking place at hyper speed. Previously accepted norms, customs, traditions, ideals, and practices are questioned as never before. The status quo is under attack.

Dr. Knight emphasized that today institutions and individuals have the opportunity to make decisions in areas which previously were not open to alternatives. In the "good old days" people had fewer choices than we have today. Many decisions, he said, were simply made by those in authority. However, over the years this has changed. Today people have more control over the decisions which affect their lives and a wider range of choices. Dr. Knight said that he teaches young people to be aware that we always have choices regardless of the situation and that how we decide among those choices is very important to our success.

I went through all of grade school and most of high school avoiding making the hard choice, not knowing the power of focusing intentional behavior. Life is loaded with challenges. You can either run from the difficulties in life or you can meet them head on with a well-thought out game plan. I am now willing to take life on, to act on it and become the team leader I so desperately want to become.

A driving purpose of playing basketball next season is for me to learn to lead at the highest level I'm capable of. I want to build a foundation for future success as a leader long after my playing days end. My behavior will be focused and intentional. I know that me and my teammates—sorry, my teammates and I—can achieve far beyond our horizons in ways we've never explored. Taylor says many people never really know the full range of their potential because too often they limit themselves to what they have seen others accomplish.

I've learned that succeeding as team leader is not a matter of chance. It's a matter of choice. Becoming an effective team leader isn't something I hope happens. It is something that will happen by daily preparation and my commitment to a deliberate action plan, leadership actions determined by the choices I make.

My cell phone rang. The generic ring-tone suggested a person that's never called me. It was Dan Hutchings. "Hi Drew."

I asked Dan if he'd have time to meet with me and Taylor later today. He said he'd be glad to and that he was sorry for his actions toward me the last month of the season.

"Hi Taylor, Drew here. Can you meet me and Dan Hutchings at McDonald's?" Taylor and I meet once a month at McDonald's to watch how parents interact with their kids. We evaluate their leadership skills in an environment in which the kids clearly have the upper hand. We also study the service crew for leadership skills, looking for leadership moments when the McDonald's team demonstrates notable acts of leadership. We pay particular attention to how the workers handle adversity. Taylor's been doing this for two years! I'm new to this game. But I'm learning a lot by observing.

We'd recently asked the McDonald's manager if she'd share with us some leadership strategies. With a smile and a couple of milkshakes she spent an hour talking to us about leadership. She said that practice improves leadership skills. Practice improves one's confidence to lead. That whether you are interested in playing soccer or performing heart surgery, it is through practice that you program yourself to succeed. She also said that when we program ourselves to lead and succeed we unleash a desire to make it happen.

The manager carefully instructed us that failure should not be seen as a bad thing, something that's not a part of leadership. She said that it is a *crucial* component of learning to lead. As student-athletes we risk failing in front of our teammates. She said many of the young leaders she mentors at her McDonald's prefer to surrender rather than risk failure. They tell themselves "I don't have the ability to succeed." She says it is her job as a leader to help them change their self-talk, to change their inner dialogue. Kinda sounds to me like Mr. Carter's instruction to help teammates believe in themselves.

We learned that at McDonald's young people are encouraged to become leaders. The manager says she asks employees during their performance review a key question. She said she asks each employee, "What if you truly decided to see yourself as a leader right now, rather than waiting until later in life?" She said many young people don't see themselves as leaders.

She explained that part of the reason is that from the time we're small children we've really only been exposed to one style of leadership. We have been taught by the model of our parents, teachers, and coaches that leadership is about trying to change and control the behavior of other people, that leadership and authority go hand in hand. She said the "default" leadership style for most people is that of an order-giver order-taker relationship which can squash a young person's natural motivation to grow and develop. Rarely, she concluded, are young people nurtured to make decisions, set standards, and develop judgment. And so most young people struggle to become leaders.

After our meeting with the manager at McDonald's I really got to thinking. What if all my teammates and I took seriously our responsibility to inspire others and invested time to build positive, meaningful relationships with teammates and our classmates? I think if we all act this way we can change our world.

Oh ya, just so you know, observing leadership moments at McDonald's is an example of focused intentional behavior. We go to McDonald's with the intention of learning lessons in leadership by focusing on what leaders do, *or don't do*. And we take notes. That's focused intentional behavior!

Dan arrived at the same time I did. Taylor was already sitting in a booth. It figures

"Hi guys," said Taylor as she looked up from her notebook. "I'm making a list of deliberate leadership actions that we'll need to take to build team cohesiveness," she said with a simple smile. I copied the list in my notebook.

Leadership Lesson 5: Focusing Intentional Behavior

> - Work with teammates to create a climate of trust
> - Encourage teammates to participate in team building exercises
> - Invite and encourage quiet or passive teammates to become involved
> - Be willing to listen and accept teammates for who they are
> - Help teammates to achieve their individual goals
> - Help teammates settle conflicts
> - Hold Saturday evening team meetings

"Dan, you're gonna have to get a leadership notebook. It's mandatory to becoming a team leader," I said as I finished my notes. Taylor reached into her book bag and pulled out a brand-new black three-ring binder and gave it to Dan. "Dan," Taylor said laughing, "here's a leadership notebook for you. I've already copied some notes to get you started." She must be the most relentless leader in the world. She's so focused and intentional. She has a notebook ready for Dan! It figures.

It's obvious that Taylor enjoys her role as a mentor. And I really appreciate her for seeing in me what I didn't know existed. She said we need to step up our pace of learning. That we need to help our coaching staff create an environment that supports leadership learning opportunities for everyone on our team.

"Guys, let me jump start the next phase of your leadership journey," said Taylor. "Here's my Leadership FIRST learning strategy," she said as she handed us a laminated notecard to remind us to develop a leadership mindset and of our commitment to becoming team leaders. On the notecard was an acrostic outlining her Leadership FIRST learning program:

Focus on priorities
Implement deliberate actions
Reflect on results
Seek feedback from teammates and coaches
Take ownership of what you learn

Dan and I agreed to apply the Leadership FIRST learning strategy every day. We now know what priorities to focus on: building right relationships, guiding with influence, initiating change, inspiring shared purpose, and focusing intentional behavior. We have a winning game plan for becoming high-performing team leaders! I'm looking forward to continuing my Leadership Quest.

Leadership Development Exercises

Leading Self
- How would I like to change the world for myself and my teammates?

Leading Others
- A teammate is talking to a friend. He/she says, "I'm really not interested in building relationships with most of my teammates." What would you do?

Leading with Others
- Call a team meeting. With your teammates discuss personal goals (academic and athletic) and team goals. Find areas where individual goals and team goals might come into conflict.

Leadership Lesson 5: Focusing Intentional Behavior

Work together to resolve any conflicts of interest that arise.

Leadership Actions that Lead to Focusing Intentional Behavior

- Exhibit a strong sense of mission
- Help align individual goals with team goals
- Establish clear performance expectations, goals, and behaviors
- Maintain high standards
- Persevere through failure and adversity
- Manage the environment
- Take positive steps
- Test yourself and your teammates

Chapter 8

Conclusion

I'd like to tell you that we won the state championship. We didn't. We did win our conference and region. Our final record was 22-8. Leadership made a huge difference.

Dan Hutchings finished the season with some outstanding offers to continue playing at some great colleges. All the coaches recruiting him said they want him to play for their school because he's a leader. Dan and I spent the whole summer learning about and practicing leadership. We joined Taylor in her monthly meetings with Mr. Carter and Coach Collins. And I took Dan to meet Dr. Knight. Dr. Knight invited us to several leadership seminars put on by some of the leading thinkers on leadership. He also introduced us to some professional athletes that were interested in learning about our Leadership Quest!

Terrell Davis finished his senior season an academic All-American. He took a leadership position with a Wall Street firm. Says he's interested in demonstrating how character and effective leadership are inseparable.

We've graduated from studying leadership at McDonald's. Taylor, Dan, and I, now study leadership at the local airport. With all that activity going on in the airport we find a least a dozen leadership lessons each time we meet there. Don't laugh. You should try it.

I've shed my Captain Complacent cape. I no longer wait until I'm told what to do, nor do I wait until later, tomorrow, next week, sometime, or someday to get things done. I look for leadership opportunities daily. And I find them, act on them, and learn. As a team leader, I'm always looking for ways to take actions that motivate and inspire my teammates by providing meaning and challenge in all that we do.

My Leadership Quest has so far been an exhilarating journey. It is important to believe in what you're doing, to have faith in your abilities. The growth I've achieved, the courage and confidence I've gained, the skill and knowledge I've acquired, these are things that can never be taken away from me.

Taylor and I went to the prom. Together! She leaves tomorrow for West Point. I think she'll fit in just fine. Don't you?

THE ACADEMY FOR SPORT LEADERSHIP

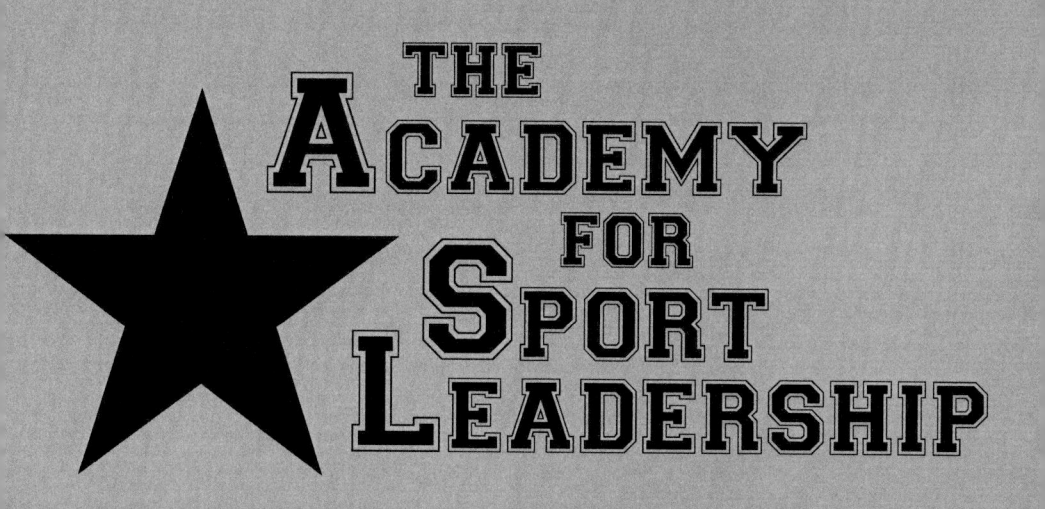

Be Prepared. Get Ready to Lead

eadership Cases

Leadership Quest

The Academy for Sport Leadership
Leadership Development Model

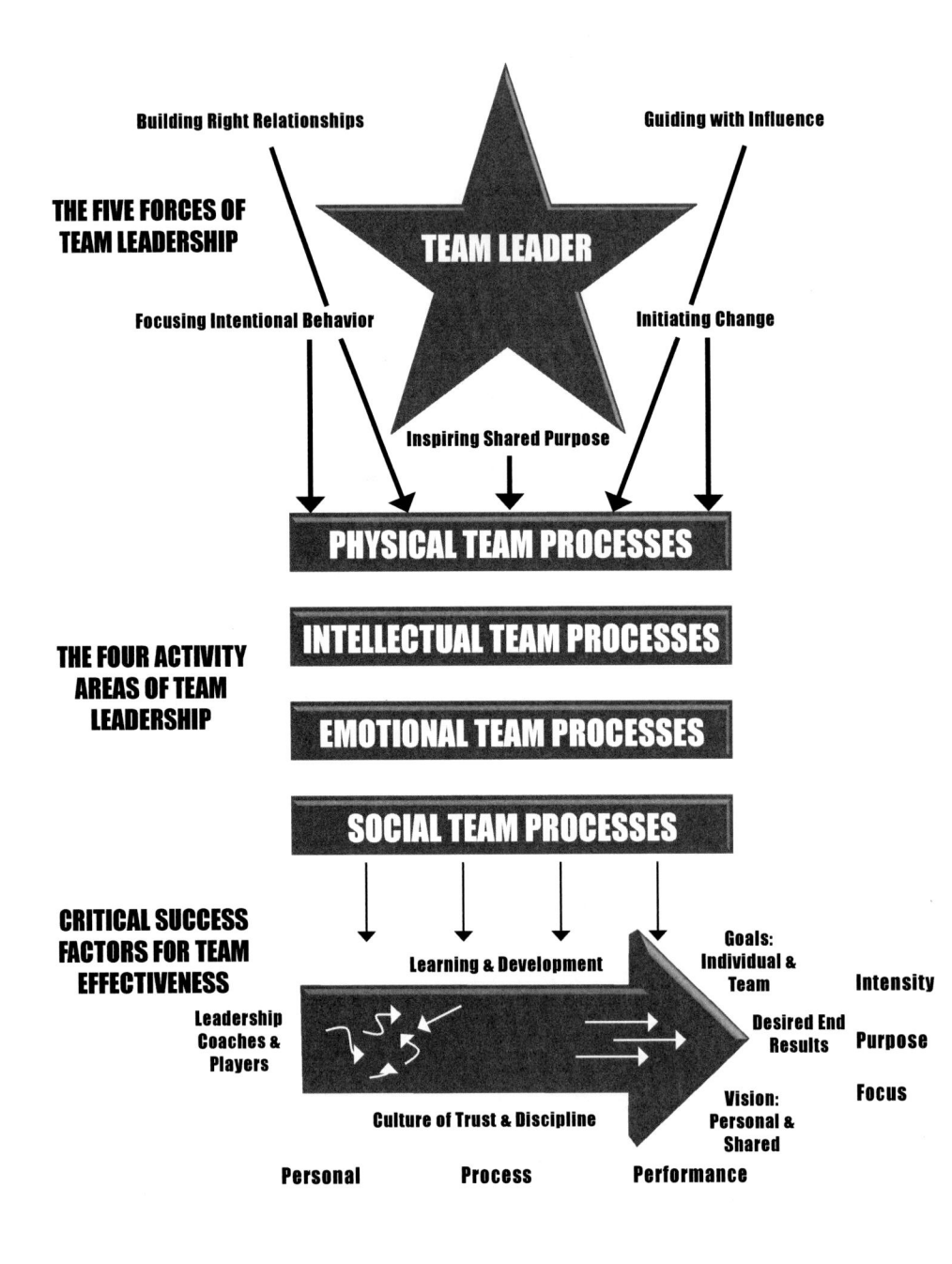

THE FIVE FORCES OF TEAM LEADERSHIP

- Building Right Relationships
- Guiding with Influence
- Focusing Intentional Behavior
- Initiating Change
- Inspiring Shared Purpose

TEAM LEADER

THE FOUR ACTIVITY AREAS OF TEAM LEADERSHIP

- PHYSICAL TEAM PROCESSES
- INTELLECTUAL TEAM PROCESSES
- EMOTIONAL TEAM PROCESSES
- SOCIAL TEAM PROCESSES

CRITICAL SUCCESS FACTORS FOR TEAM EFFECTIVENESS

- Leadership Coaches & Players
- Learning & Development
- Culture of Trust & Discipline
- Goals: Individual & Team
- Desired End Results
- Vision: Personal & Shared
- Intensity
- Purpose
- Focus

Personal Process Performance

58

Team Leadership Cases

Developing Social and Emotional Intelligence

Case Study	5 Forces of Leadership •• See ASL Model ••	Leadership Topics	Skills
The Final Push	Building Right Relationships & Focusing Intentional Behavior	Culture of Trust	Initiating trust building behaviors
Code of Honor or Code of Silence	Building Right Relationships & Guiding with Influence	Ethics	Resolving Conflict
Winning Isn't the Only Thing	Guiding with Influence & Inspiring Shared Purpose	Emotional Intelligence	Motivating Self and Others
The Pecking Order	Building Right Relationships & Guiding with Influence	Leadership Power and influence	Team Building
This May Hurt a Little	Building Right Relationships & Focusing Intentional Behavior	Leadership Communication	Leading Conversations and Discussion
Big "We," little "me"	Initiating Change & Inspired Shared Purpose	The Leader as a Relationship Builder	Creating Team Cohesiveness
Initiating Change that Endures	Initiating Change & Guiding with Influence	Change	Giving and Receiving Peer Feedback
Didn't See the Cliff Coming	Building Right Relationships & Initiating Change	Leadership Communication	Handling Team Conflict
Don't Rock the Boat	Guiding with Influence & Initiating Change	Shaping Culture and Values	Communication Handling
United We Stand, Divided We Can't Stand Each Other	Building Right Relationships & Inspired Shared Purpose	Shaping Culture and Values	Problem Solving Listening

Case Analysis

Case Preparation for Discussion

The Academy for Sport Leadership's short case studies are designed to provide you and your teammates a tool for learning personal skills such as self-awareness and assertive speaking, and interpersonal skills such as listening, conflict resolution and collaborative problem solving. The case resolution is less about specific actions than it is about intentionally engaging with teammates to both speak and really hear, to both influence and be influenced.

Case Analysis Process
1. Read the case and respond to the questions
2. State the central issue.
3. Develop reasonable courses of action. Think of this as "Preplay."
4. With small group or team evaluate alternative courses of action.

Your main objective is not only to read the case and come to some conclusions and reasonable courses of action, but to be prepared to discuss with your teammates. If you and your teammates discuss openly and really listen to one another, you'll have taken a few giant steps in the direction of creating a cohesive team.

Case Study

Before you read each case do the following:
   In the upper left hand corner of the case study place:
   D1 = Disappointment
   In the upper right hand corner of the case study place:
   D2 = Disagreement

As you read the case do the following:
   Place a D1 or a D2 next to the all the phrases or sentences that you think highlight either the possibility of **disappointment** on the behalf of team members, or the potential for **disagreement** on facts and perceptions. There is no right or wrong answer, just what you think is the best fit with the scenario presented.

   For Example, here's a sentence from the case study *The Pecking Order*: "However, at the urging of Cheyanne she began to exert her power over the non-starters." You might choose to place a D1 next to this assertion as a result of your assessment that Cheyanne's teammates might be disappointed with this behavior.

   The principle purpose of the case study is to help you improve leadership skills such as speaking, listening, judgment, and conflict resolution. As a team you will improve your collective performance to solve a wide-range of interpersonal problems.

   A desired outcome of analyzing a case with your teammates is that you'll get to know them at a deeper level. That is, you're teammates will share their beliefs, values, assumptions, feelings, motives, perceptions, and so will you. When this happens you get an inner view of one another.

The Final Push

Relationship Building and Accountability to the Team

On the Wednesday before the third game of the season Breanna twisted her ankle in practice. While cutting in front of a defender as she was chasing down the ball a teammate initiated her awkward fall by slightly shoving her on the hip.

Emily witnessed the "accident." Earlier in the scrimmage Jennifer was embarrassed by Breanna's skillful dribbling of the ball. Breanna received a pass just outside the goal and maneuvered between Jennifer and another defender to score a goal. Jennifer, struggling to get playing time, was visibly upset. Emily was on the Blue Team just as was Jennifer. During a timeout in play shortly after Breanna's goal Jennifer commented to the other members of the Blue Team that Breanna was a "show off who thinks she's better than us." Emily brushed it off as "Jennifer just being Jennifer".

Jennifer quickly ran after the loose ball leaving Breanna writhing in pain. Tina stopped to help Breanna to her feet and carried her to the sidelines. With a stop in play the coach asked Breanna if she was okay. She'd been some distance from the incident and assumed Breanna had simply planted her foot and twisted it reaching for the ball with her other leg.

However, when Jennifer huffed under her breath "she's

faking it" to her Blue Team members Emily knew she had to take action.

Questions for Discussion

- If you're Emily, do you think it's appropriate to do something?
- What relevance is the fact that the incident took place before the third game of the season?
- Using the Academy for Sport Leadership's LDM on page 58 (Leadership Development Model), explain why Emily should do something. After clarifying the reason Emily should do something, describe what she might do to ensure the incident is handled properly.
- What are some likely consequences if Emily takes action?
- What are the likely consequences if Emily decides not to take action?

What's at Stake?

What happens when we fail to build right relationships? Things you hoped *wouldn't* happen do happen—and they occur with greater frequency and at the most inopportune moments.

Point to Ponder
Team learning leads to the development of shared mental models leading to clarity of communication, consistency of action, and commitment to the team.

The Code of Silence or a Code of Honor?
The Certainty of Silence Over the Risk of Speaking Up

Aaron was satisfied with his performance. He'd just pitched a shutout and his team won its fifth game in a row to take control of second place in their division. On the ride home Jamaal was playing cards with Aaron when he dropped a bomb on Aaron. Several teammates were involved in criminal activity—they were stealing electronic equipment from a local store. The teammates had a friend that worked the night shift at the store and would invite them to "drop in" and leave with a few things without paying for them.

Aaron was taken by surprise. He would never have suspected that Dane and Glenn would involve themselves in criminal activity. As teammates last year he assumed that they were student-athletes with high values. Aaron asked Jamaal how he found out. He said that Glenn asked him if he wanted to go "shopping" Friday night. Glenn described to Jamaal how he and Dane had gotten well over $1000 worth of electronics. Jamaal told Aaron he brushed it off and told Glenn he had something else to do.

Aaron and Jamaal were bound by the *team's Code of Honor* to not lie, cheat, or deceive, nor to tolerate anyone on the team who did. Glenn was the starting center fielder and an All-Conference player last season. Dane was a reserve infielder. Both players were contributing to the team's success.

Questions for Discussion

- Why do you think people tend to grow up with the norm of a "code of silence" in situations involving the indiscretions of others?
- Why do you think Jamaal told Aaron about their teammate's indiscretions?
- If you were Aaron would you tell Jamaal that "I never heard a word from you"?
- What are the likely consequences if Aaron fails to take action?
- What is a likely consequence if the coach finds out?
- If the players are dismissed from the team, how would you as a team leader re-group your teammates?
- What types of "off the field" incidents have you witnessed during your playing career? What did you do?
- Why is there certainty in silence while risk in speaking up?

What's at Stake?

From a position of honor and integrity we are committed to act. From a position of loyalty we sometimes feel compelled to *not* act. This seeming dilemma can cause anguish, anger, and apathy. In the end, one must choose which is greater, misplaced loyalty or acting with integrity and honor.

Point to Ponder
Any violation of honesty and integrity, however seemingly small, saps your ethical strength, leaving you weaker for the tough challenges you're going to face sooner or later. Another Point to Ponder: Do you learn best by experiencing examples of loyal behavior, or by being betrayed?

Winning Isn't the Only Thing

Learning from Setbacks

It was the final game of a lousy season. We had won the first three games, beating Burberry, Lesser, and Schultz Valley, but then lost the next dozen games, four of them by a single goal. So we badly wanted to win this last one at the Davis arena against our archrival Paul S. Brown High. As co-captain of the team I had scored a good amount of goals so far during the season, and we were feeling pretty good about our chances.

It was a good game. We pushed Brown into overtime at 2-2.

But very quickly, the other team scored and we lost again, for the eighth time in a row. In a fit of frustration, I flung my hockey stick across the ice of the arena, skated after it, and headed back to the locker room. The team was already there, taking off their skates and uniforms. All of a sudden, the door opened and Coach Thaler strode in.

The locker room fell silent. Every eye was glued on the veteran coach, one who'd had great success at the school.

Case Study

Questions for Discussion

- Why might a player lose their self-confidence during a losing streak?
- How can this impact the team?
- Can a single player losing their self-confidence affect others?
- What does confidence give you?
- How can you help teammates build self-confidence?
- How might a disheartening loss or consecutive losses affect a team's collective confidence?
- In what ways can a player help others fight through a battle with self doubt?
- How might you and your teammates search for leadership lessons in setbacks?

What's at Stake?

Building self-confidence in others is a vital part of leadership. It comes from providing opportunities and challenges for people to do things they never imagined they could do. Self-confident players inspire confidence in their teammates and gaining the confidence of your teammates is one of the ways in which you can contribute to your team's success.

Point to Ponder
Losing is a part of sports. Losing is a part of winning. If you don't know how to lose, you'll never know how to win.

The Pecking Order

An Introduction to Status and Leadership

Pecking Order: A hierarchical system of social organization.

By the end of preseason Emily was convinced that the rest of the team would follow her wherever she went. She worked hard, was the best player on the team, excelled in the classroom, and most players really liked her. It was obvious to her and Cheyanne, her closest friend on the team, that she was the center of this group of student-athletes. Cheyanne, with the status as Emily's best friend, was viewed by their teammates as the "second in charge."

Like the characters in the book *Lord of the Flies* the girls arranged themselves into a hierarchy—a manifestation of their subconscious life experience. A sorting of team membership by playing status gave clarity to who to look to for leadership, friendship, and followership. It seemed as if each player was comfortable with their place in the "naturally" arranged order.

In the past Emily didn't really recognize the ease with which her teammates willingly followed her every word, her every action. However, at the urging of Cheyanne she began to exert her power over the non-starters. On road trips she would alter seating arrangements on the bus. She engineered the "selection" of lockers and managed to convince the team that this was a vital way for relationships to flourish.

Who Rules the Roost?

The concept of a 'pecking order' was coined back in the 1920s by biologists who discovered that chickens maintain a hierarchy with one chicken pecking another of lower status. In the absence of a rooster, one particular chicken will dominate all others. Every henhouse has a pecking order which is established early on and then again if a new chicken is introduced to the roost.

The 'pecking order' concept was used to explain similar behavior in organizations by humans in the 1950s and is a regular topic of study in the social sciences. A pecking order generally is used to describe hierarchy in an organizational setting. For example, the principal is "higher" in the pecking order than the assistant principal. And the college president is higher in the pecking order than the dean of instruction. Is there a pecking order on your team?

Questions for Discussion

- Why do you think a pecking order might naturally emerge in a sports team context?
- Do student-athletes (in particular, you and your teammates) care if a pecking order exists?
- What are the advantages of a pecking order? Disadvantages?
- How does a pecking order determine who people communicate and interact with?
- How can a team deal with the negative effects of a dysfunctional pecking order?

What's at Stake?

Social influence refers to attempts to affect or change other people. However, when that influence is based on the ability to threaten or punish teammates problems are likely to occur.

Point to Ponder
Learning how to act assertively, rather than passively or aggressively, is a desired trait of fearless leaders and followers.

This May Hurt a Little

Trying to Turn the Tide

Coming off a tough loss Andrae knew he needed to get inside the heads of his teammates. As a team leader he felt responsible for providing his teammates with a reality check. He wanted to make sure everyone understood the truth that was evident in the last game. Andrae was aware that often times the truth hurts, but he was certain it was time to tell the truth.

After practice on Friday Andrae corralled his teammates in the locker room. Andrae, a respected team leader quietly asked everyone to take a seat. Several players grudgingly asked why and Andrae simply said "Come on."

"What I saw on Wednesday, I've never seen a team play with such a lack of enthusiasm, lack of effort. Even when we had a chance to win, the energy and body language wasn't there. No one stepped up to meet that challenge," said Andrea. "The energy I saw, it didn't seem like there was a sense of energy from anybody. No one seemed to want it. You want to go in there with a purpose. You have to want it. I saw none of that."

An uncooperative teammate quickly became defensive. "So you're blaming everyone else for our loss? Man, why don't you think before you speak?" Andrae recognized the meeting could go in a different direction if he responded defensively or pointed a finger of blame.

Questions for Discussion

- What in this case is relevant to your current team situation?
- What are the differences between performance and effort?
- How does Andrae know with certainty what the problem is?
- Why is it important that Andrae act quickly?
- Should Andrae involve anyone else in his analysis of the problem?
- Why is it often said that "The truth hurts"?
- How do you and your teammates *tell the truth*?
- How would you suggest handling defensiveness by a teammate?

What's at Stake?

Team cohesion refers to the interpersonal bonds that hold a team together. Members of a cohesive team are more likely to accept confrontation and conflict that helps the team meet its goals. Low levels of team cohesion limit the team's ability to work together and decrease a team's capacity to overcome adversity.

Point to Ponder
The problem is rarely the problem. The response to the problem invariably ends up being the problem.

Big "We," little "me"

Thinking and Acting Like a Teammate

Erin arrived late to her first class of the day. She was still brooding about not playing in last night's game. Consumed with disappointment in her coaches, teammates, and herself, Erin was contemplating quitting the team. She reflected on the hours upon hours invested over the past two years simply to eke out a few minutes of playing time each game. She'd set high goals for herself, and she met most of them. She improved in the weight room and on the playing field. She always gave all she had in practice and the coaches were usually pleased with her as a member of the team. However, she seemed to be stuck on starting. Playing time. Seemed little else mattered to her. She wasn't quite sure why she felt this way, she'd always thought of herself as a very good teammate. She enjoyed working alongside everyone, had not grudges and couldn't muster a bad word about her teammates. She just wanted to play. And she'd just realized after last night's game she really wouldn't get much playing time this year—her senior season.

Questions for Discussion

- Why might a team member become discouraged about a lack of playing time?
- How can you encourage teammates to balance "Me" with "We?"
- How might you unknowingly discourage a teammate from accepting "we?"
- How might Erin's thoughts determine her behavior?
- What happens when one team member goes in his or her own direction?
- What might happen when a team member places too much emphasis on themselves?
- What are the benefits of being a member of a team? (physically, intellectually, emotionally, socially)
- What "rewards" might a player receive that doesn't get much playing time?

What's at Stake?

While we all have to take responsibility for ourselves and our success in life, we need to do so in a way that honors the various wholes of which we are a part. Thinking and acting "BIG We, little me" is not about denying yourself, your needs, or your individuality. It is about realizing that you are part of a whole that is greater than you.

Point to Ponder
A popular proverb states,
"The best potential in 'me' is 'we.'"

Case Study

Initiating Change that Endures

Creating a Context for a Cohesive Team

David, a senior, was getting set for his final season. He felt that his chance had finally come to fill the vacuum left by Peter Brown, last year's team leader. For David it was an honor to be chosen by his teammates to be the team captain. Just as Peter did last season, David knew one of the first things he had to do was to initiate change. Peter's strength the previous season was as a Social Leader. David was concerned that while competent as a social leader, his real strength is as an Emotional Leader.

The first practice of the preseason was approaching. While working out with several of his teammates he asked each to provide him their view of where the team was emotionally. Specifically, where was the team emotionally at the end of last season and where is it now. David's concern was that since the season ended without the team making the playoffs—after expecting to go deep into the playoffs—the returning players might have lost some confidence in the coaching staff and the capabilities of the team. David wanted to set the tone early, but knew that it was important to know how his teammates were thinking about the upcoming season.

After the informal workout with his teammates, David became concerned. The three players he "interviewed" regarding the emotional state of the teams' members revealed a sense of pessimism. The lack of optimism was based largely on the loss of Peter and several stand-out players. David's teammates voiced concern for the physical capabilities of the current players and noted that while Peter tried desperately last year to help create a cohesive team, it seemed to them that the team never truly came together. Their lack of confidence stemmed from the feeling, and the evidence that suggested they were not going to be a very good team.

David understood that he had a challenge in front of him. The practice habits and mind-set that lead to high achievement for individuals and teams was likely to suffer if he didn't take action quickly. David didn't know where to begin. He wondered if he should begin with a commitment to a mission or if he should look for a way for his teammates to identify barriers to change and performance.

Questions for Discussion

- Do you think David feels the need to "live" up to the standards Peter demonstrated last year?
- What actions might David take to initiate a change in the emotional state of his teammates?
- What are the likely consequences if David doesn't take action?
- What are some likely consequences if David's actions fail?
- How should David respond to teammates that resist change?
- What are a couple of things David might do to gain commitment to the team from those teammates that are "less" committed to the team?

What's at Stake?

The best team leaders lead with honesty, humility, and understand their value system. They provide leadership, vision, and spirit that produces perseverance—especially in the face of adversity.

Point to Ponder
We either move towards others, away from others or against others. When we believe that others are our adversaries, we move against them. As soon as we see and feel that others are moving away from us we respond instinctively to let them go their own way.

I Didn't See the Cliff Coming

Sometimes We Don't Tell the Truth Because We're Not Sure How

Danielle Hale stood in the upstairs hall of the dimly lit building waiting for Tonja, her teammate, to arrive. The darkness into which she stared was hopelessly empty of light and all else. She'd been disappointed once again by the comments several teammates made to her during the road trip. She wasn't sure why they were saying such negative things about her.

Led by Tonja, a small clique was developing. Danielle, a team captain last season recognized that Tonja was doing some dishonest things to become the team's leader. It was clear to Danielle, however, that Tonja was leading teammates in a direction that was tearing the team apart.

Tonja turned the corner in the hall and approached Danielle. She did so with fury and anger. "What's the problem Hale?" Danielle, knowing that Tonja wouldn't be receptive said, "We need to talk."

Danielle had been avoiding this conflict, ignoring it for some time now. She wasn't sure how to tell Tonja the truth of how her talking behind her back hurt her and how she was leading teammates in the wrong direction.

Case Study

Questions for Discussion

- Why is a lack of conflict potentially a sign of a problem?
- Why is it important to solve internal conflicts and disagreements?
- How important is it to get to know your teammates thoughts and feelings?
- What happens when team members *don't* treat each other with respect?
- What social skills are necessary for team members to confront one another with the truth?
- Why do we sometimes feel vulnerable when telling the truth?
- Is it usually true that "The longer we work together, the better we get along"?
- What might you do to confront a teammate that is saying untrue things about another teammate?

What's at Stake?

One "small" incident can distort a relationship. A series of such incidents can damage a relationship beyond repair. Sometimes we hesitate telling the truth to others for fear we will hurt their feelings or ruin a relationship irreparably. Sometimes we don't tell the truth because we're not sure how. And yet, the benefits of relating to others through shared accountability and openness far outweigh the risks.

Point to Ponder
Developing a healthy solution to a conflict requires open communication, respect for the other side, and a creative search for mutually satisfying alternatives.

Don't Rock the Boat

The Pressure to Conform

Angelo walked quickly through the locker room. He felt a little out of place as none of his new teammates had yet to step forward and make him feel welcomed. Oh, they all said hello and "glad to have you as a part of the team" at the kickoff lunch. But not one teammate took the time to find out who he was and how he was doing. It was early in the pre-season so he just figured that his teammates were just getting used to one another.

A few weeks later Angelo still felt like an outsider. Funny thing, he never saw his teammates expressing much interest in each other—outside of their small 2-3 person groups. Intrigued by the strange feeling he was getting from the stand-offish attitude toward interpersonal interaction on the team, he asked Solomon about the lack of relationships among the members of the team. Solomon, took him outside the locker room and put his arm around Angleo.

Solomon in a low tone told Angleo that "three general rules apply." He carefully counted them off. "One. Take care of your own personal needs. Two. If you disagree with any of the veterans on the team, it is best not to say so. And three, keep your distance from Jordin and Jesse."

Case Study

Questions for Discussion

- How would you react in this kind of team culture?
- Why do people have a need for a sense of connection and belonging?
- What are some ways teammates earn one another's trust?
- How would you build rapport in this environment?
- What are some possible risks of "violating" Solomon's three general rules?
- What are some potential benefits of "violating" Solomon's three general rules?
- Many interpersonal conflicts stay unresolved. What is the likelihood of resolving a conflict in this environment? Why?

What's at Stake?

We conform not because we are weak, but because the status quo is a default path we are used to following. If you are committed to making your team a healthy one, you need to have the courage to take risks and engage in passionate dialogue about personal and team success.

Point to Ponder
Members of cohesive teams trust one another on an emotional level, and they are comfortable being vulnerable with each other about their weaknesses, mistakes, disagreements, and fears.

United We Stand, Divided We Can't Stand Each Other
Lessons for Facing the Reality of Team Life

Junior forward, Malcolm Bodaken, slammed the ball down and watched as it bounced across the field. "I hate these jerks!"

He was clearly angry and frustrated that a teammate did not pass him the ball while he was wide open. This was the third time during the practice that Roberto or Conner, both seniors, failed to deliver the ball to him in scoring position. Malcolm felt this subtle "icing" had been going on for over a week now. In fact, when he asked Robert and Conner several days prior to this incident both suggested they simply make decisions based on what they see happening on the field.

Jeremy pulled Malcolm aside and tried to calm his teammate. Malcolm, an emotional player, was prone to outbursts punctuated by shouting and sulking. His blowups usually lasted only a minute or two. However, they always had a lingering effect on his teammates. Malcolm blasted Jeremy. "Trust me, this is something those guys have been doing for some time!" Jeremy didn't know who "those guys" were, but it didn't matter. He was the first to arrive "on the scene" and therefore was expected to get his teammate under control. As a Wildcat he knew "That's the way we do it here." Malcolm continued his tirade while

Case Study

the team looked on. Jeremy walked away and went back to the practice.

In the locker room, forty-five minutes removed from the incident, Jeremy took Malcolm aside. "You said 'those guys' have been doing something to you. Can you tell me who 'they' are and what it is they're doing?" Malcolm, still frustrated but controlling his smoldering anger explained his observation and suspicion that Conner and Roberto were trying to keep him from scoring and improving his performance.

Questions for Discussion

- As a team leader how will you engage your teammates with the question "How can we solve this problem"?
- What is the major challenge for Malcolm?
- What are the key factors in this incident that might help you find an effective solution?
- If teammates don't like each other what might you do to help them find common ground?
- Was Malcolm rational in his perspective? How might you better understand his perspective?

What's at Stake?

We're all familiar with the leadership slogan "United we stand, divided we fall." This motto echoes the fundamental truth that loyalty is a cornerstone of successful teams. How do individual relationships effect a team's cohesiveness?

Point to Ponder
The values of the world around us and the people we surround ourselves with have a profound effect on shaping who we are and who we become.

RESOURCES TO HELP YOU ON YOUR LEADERSHIP QUEST

I hope you enjoyed reading about Drew and Taylor's journey to becoming team leaders. If you've decided to begin your leadership quest I applaud you. When you become a leader you'll change your world. To help you succeed in your leadership quest we encourage you to take advantage of the many resources for student-athletes developed by The Academy for Sport Leadership. The Academy's resources will help you develop a leadership mindset and build your leadership skill set.

Leadership Quest

If you've been inspired by the Leadership Quest philosophy in this book and want to build a team leadership program that will change your world please contact The Academy for Sport Leadership.

To book a Leadership Quest presentation for your school or program, please contact The Academy for Sport Leadership.

The Leadership Quest is available at a special price on bulk orders for schools, colleges, universities, clubs and not-for-profit community groups. To order contact The Academy for Sport Leadership info@sportleadership.com.

The Academy for Sport Leadership
www.sportleadership.com